Seven to Nine

John Gordon

BookLeaf Publishing

Presentation by *BookLeaf Publishing*

Web: www.bookleafpub.com

E-mail: info@bookleafpub.com

ISBN :9789357699303

First edition 2022

DEDICATION

To my closest dearest friends - thanks for putting up with me

PREFACE

"Such aching mystery hides, in your stardust-glimmer eyes" - John Mark-Greene.

She is Her

Purity flows from her soul like waters
Innocence radiates like the bright summer sun
But is all as it seems.

While her smile may be angelic
Beneath lurks sensual malice
That would drive all to sin.

In public she shines like a lamp on a hill
For all to see, and in private solitude
She facilitates and dominates all desires.

She is a rare and wonderful creature
Everyone who reads her often misjudges
Book covers aren't the whole story.

Human descriptions cannot merely be
Restrained by mere mortal dialogue
As humans are more beautiful than we will ever
understand.

New Glasses

New glasses - faded eyes glisten
The iris' shine like long lost diamonds
And stare out for rose tint and nostalgia towers.

No more rosy pink or familiar shades
Now a morose and ghastly leprosy white
Which clings to lungs like lonely limpets.

Comfort comes from beautiful music
I can still hear from ages before
When years and life were easier.

Watchless hands tell of no years
Spent alone or waiting for that wondrous
epiphany
Now left with darkness and an abyss.

What is brave?

Bravery means what?
What does it stand for?
Where in the world does bravery still count?

In our existence, of newspaper coated walls,
We watch, eyes wide like cats
Waiting for what cowardice is brought like
cream in a saucer.

The braver the messenger, the less believable the
message
In our minds, we exist like molecules in a drop
of water,
Scrutinised, as Wells said, in a microscopic
manner.

Where have all the good ones gone?
Buried beneath sleaze, beneath the arches of the
time
Gone, gone the form of bravery - rise the demon
of falsehoods and pain.

Been to a party? Tell the truth!
Borrowed money? No judgement here!
Messed around? Well....I won't tell if you won't -
but to be brave one must!

In our brave new world, the restart has failed
System crashed and burned like Fokker's did in WW1,
With flaming engines roaring and howling calls of "no confidence".

So the scared new world (un nouveaux mond peur) struggles through
Suffocating the bravery and throttling the truth with the same bloody rope it hangs itself.

Empty Spaces and Dark Gaps

I sit alone in my quiet apartment, drink in hand,
and I begin to understand why we
split. When we met in that darkened club we
somehow could see the sparks fly, and feel
breezes sigh and I began to wonder why, and
whether our love was true; and whether you
were true to your word, or just oblivious to it,
and just in it for the sex.

Okay, our lives were never supposed to fit
together as we were too different. There is now
an empty space in the bed next to me, and once
again I feel oh so lonely.
This pain within grows wider and bigger, and it
seems like some demented digger is hell
bent on finishing the hole, deep deep down
within my soul. The dark gaps begin to
show, and then I realise the empty spaces are for
the faces we loved, lost and clung to
when we needed someone to rely on, a sturdy
shoulder for us to cry upon.

Yes, we were different, and I'm sad we parted,
but our love wasn't meant to have even
been started. Casual meetings in public places,
the sweet perfume of yours that gave

such brilliant embraces, and the times we snuck away from the noise and poise of social snobbery and just sat on the rooftops gazing across at the skyline with ease.
That first kiss you planted on my cold lips, the first touch on my shoulder from your delicate fingertips sent shivers down my spine and as I thought to myself, all is going to be fine; the warm passion, the hot irrationality began to sear through our veins.

I sit now and think of the passionate warmth you brought into my life. The warmth similar to a fire on cold winter's nights, you warmed my soul and took away the pain. Again, again and again, we rose bursting with passion long thought dead inside, then together we did ride on a mixture of ecstatic joy and passionate love until we realised that the beautiful girl and boy were so alike it had been designated from above. As you pulled me closer, I felt a voice whisper to me, she is no one night romance or evening passion, you must have her, claim her, crave her! For goodness sakes man, she needs you and you need her. So put your hands where you can see them!

By the time I did, she was gone, and the gaps began to show again. I felt that tight pain

deep within my aching chest, the pain of loss as
yet another hole was being dug deep
within my soul. Those empty spaces and dark
gaps are sometimes self-provoked.

Cup of Revolution

How does a man think he can shape a new world? What levels can he go to without causing pain or destruction to those he is trying to help? With the tools he has, how can he define himself as a rebel?

Just sit down. Relax. Have a cup of tea.

Amidst all the bustle and banging on the city, somewhere, dark, dank and lonely, our rebel begins to brew and plot. He has just been put into the boiling environment around him. It seems hot and steamy at first, but he soon becomes used to the temperature and adjusts.

Slowly, but surely, he spreads his words like the rats spread the bubonic plague in the 15th Century. There are more people turning to listen, and they too become enraptured and stirred into a frenzy of different ideas and their minds are soon cluttered with new flavours, colours and ideas.

And yet from this, some of the revolutionaries try to sweeten it. Revolution can sometimes be a bit bitter for those unused to it. But for the hardcore rebels who can withstand the heat, withstand the darkness and still stand for what is stirring within them, they want it plain and simple.

Some revolutions can be fruity, some can be built around darkness, others like dabs of sweetness, some like the bitter strong truth; but they're all boiled up and hot under the collar about something.

You might not realise it, but even you are part of this revolution. This different horizon; a place where you can discover new places, new ideas and still enjoy your morning cuppa with no worries.

Che Guevara once said "The revolution is not an apple that falls when it is ripe. You have to make it fall". Similarly with our revolution, we never know when the right time is to pour out of beliefs and to stir some seriously tasty mocca-frappa that will either satisfy, intrigue, spark interest, disgust, horrify or even arouse some people.

The time is now. The day is here. I'm just going to put the kettle on.

Day....

Ensconced and enclosed in a dystopia
Watching bread lines with 2 metre lines
Before reaching quarry or executioner's axe.

After losing touch, emotional empathy dies
The lack of connection withers the rose garden
Killing what wonder was remaining.

Khaki corduroys and white polo is a uniform
Of prisoners who reside in their stalags
Waiting for the totalitarians to boom commands.

Flounted orders go unheard like religion
Restrictions are foreign, like the EU
And a united kingdom to us.

Ignorance is no longer bliss.
Imprisonment is no longer a nightmare.
Groundhog Day was based in 2020,
Prove me wrong?!?

The Blossom Blame Game

When the blossom grows in cherry pink, winter is dead.
Where once frost and gloom, now sunshine o'erhead.

Look at how green everything is, how delicate, how new!
I am learning innocence, lying quietly by myself,
As sunshine dances around the white walls, this desk, my hands.

I am not a person, but a nameless number #072804.
I am nobody; I have nothing, but pain.
I have a name given by cruel gods and given up to society
I have a history given up to bullies and my body to gluttony.

My body drops like a pebble, and the ripples strangle.
This brings me numbness like bright needles in my swollen veins.

I am like a twenty one year old cargo ship, let
slip
Stubbornly hanging by my earlobes, dangling
over the inky mist below.

The walls around me are like warnings of eternal
death.
The blossoms should be behind bars, like
dangerous animals.
I didn't want to see spring, may I go away now?

What's Changed?

Bearded man sits in a café
Lion-headed stick at his feet
His eyes darkened with pockets of aged virtues.

His swollen hands ache and throb
And pound like coronary attacks in his
Wrists, he feels needle sharp points.

Once a placid, languid lake
Now without a fix of coffee beans
He becomes a tsunami that can destroy
Any and all in his path.

With a hole in his heart he sits alone
Never needed by any from his past
Just alone and no more dead than yesterday.

23

23 and feeling great, up and at 'em
Ready to create, the winds of time
Blast in my face and fly around me.

23 and feeling okay, another day of grey
To which the hours are years and
The positives turn into fears.

23 and feeling crap, life is nothing but a trap
Which hides gilded cages with heavy bars
If you escape, they ring alarms.

23 and nothing else, if only there was
A something to give me purpose
To save me from my black, worrisome mind.

And that...is jazz

From the words of the singer
A little flower grows slowly
Rooting itself in a harmonic blues scale.

The refrain hangs like wall art
Floating through the cigarette smoke
Of chain-smoking aficionados and beatniks.

Each click of the fingers,
Each tap of the drum can
Make the listener feel sweet and numb.

The buzz of a trumpet stings,
Like a needle at the first to the last - and baby,
That's jazz!

The Child Adult

A child was she, with pigtails
Plated, kiss curls and ringlets
Twirling as she danced around.

Innocence hasn't corrupted her
But her brain grows and her eyes
Reflect a childlike palace.

A child she has remained, yet
Frustrated and angry she is
No maturity or promise in sight.

Just realisation of growing apart
Of finding the truth to be
As painful as puberty.
What does it mean to love again?

The Mother Friend

Faded images of teenage femininity
Wiser than her years as she throws
The dolls and toys out for good.

A maternal shoulder, the loving rock
Acting as surrogate she-wolf to a hungry pack
Preparing for a future to come.

No fake mask of powder or glitter does she wear
No images for boy's twisted dirty minds did she
appear
A model of decency and clean cut figure did she
provide.

The teenage years were not for her.
She grew to prepare for a time when her friends
needed her
When the mother hen appeared to comfort her
chicks.

Some people just don't understand how
important it is
To be responsible for your actions, but how
responsibility
Doesn't have to replace having fun.

Realising the Gospels - Matthew

Because I am.
A new morning, the world begins to shine.
The moment of existence stands on ceremony.
Like a walled city.
The hilltop shines - unlike the hidden bushel world.

The bushel shrouds itself in darkness of it's mother world, but the hilltop says
"Emerge, arise, for from your branches will come fruit of wisdom and life to be enjoyed by all.
If you hide, your gifts will not grow. Instead, you will wither, weaken and rot"

"Therefore" the hilltop continued "I say unto you, humble bushel, stand your roots firm in the sunshine soil, drink deep of the golden rays and produce a rich bounty".

He's Here - In Double Trust

Mute point. Silent as the grave. In all the world,
the homosapien stand and tries to speak.
The babble of concernation, the consonants and
vowels that tumble out like teeth from a boxer's
jaw.

Crooked leer, uneven crown. Uneasy are the
states we find ourselves in.
The logs on the fire burn red, with the blood of
angry men and women alike and stink like
revolution.

Happenstance. Coincidence. Or de we, be design
face many natural shocks on life's wheel as a
macabre parlour game, planned by a delusional,
leprosy ridden God with no compassion?

Sunrise, see the sunrise. The orange and crimson
beacon of the new dawn waking - but what of
the world before?
What of the final kingdom that declares - IT IS
DONE!

WELL????????
IS IT?????????

Ferlinghetti

beat philosopher - oh great ferlinghetti!
my saviour - the one whose baritonal
melancholic vocal rings like notre dame
the true master - oh great ferlinghetti!

you survive - you thrive - you contrive
the words - sting man of wire beard and pubic
eyebrows
sting like wasp's tails, and burn like lsd acid
smells

an alto saxophone solo later and you are still
stood
in a cross - oh jehovah of poets
to mark your final stop before the pearly gates of
san francis

co! go! go! go! go! go! go!
c'mon 'n' here, this beat master go
like bongo and conga in three quarter time
ferlinghetti is here to stay!

So You've Been (insert problem here)

We've all been there
It's normal

Not really a poem - just a statement.

Use the space below: write it out.
Words flow when we're upset - try and write it -
I promise, it may help.

Herron's Lamb to Slaughter

On spook street I stand, looking for a herd of
slow horses
Reminding myself of the time that Joe Country,
was more than just a memory.
No more are the lions on the prowl from their
pride. They lie dead. Now Real Tigers, with eyes
burning bright hunt the ground, paws ready in
and around the new London rules.

(In basic terms - spies are weird)

Goodbye

Goodbye. It's been fun and we've had some good times. I feel as though it's time to leave, but in this short reprieve, I just want to think back to some of the happier times. I recall how we used to sit up until the wee small hours of the morning and talk about everything from grazed knees to the bullies at school. Times like that spent with you made my world seem such more precious and worthwhile.

Even during my darker days, you would sit beside me and recall all the good things and the praise, I had received from family and friends. You would hug me so tight that I thought I would explode, I didn't realise how much love you really showed. Now that I'm leaving and ready to move, I won't ever forget you no matter how much you may tell me to. I will call you every day and write whenever I get the chance, to hear your voice and laugh about those silly dances; dances of joy whenever I passed, but the story of a little boy who thought he couldn't be classed, as anything but a mischief maker, and a bully; you stood by me and fought for me.

Now that I'm no longer near, to comfort or hold your closer my dear, I'm writing this now to show how much I really love you. I love you mummy and I miss you loads. I'm trying now to hold back the tears, as now I feel alone with so many fears. I just want a hug and a gentle warm embrace, I want to see once more, your lovely friendly face. I love you so much and I hate to you leave you now, but I can't say the word to leave with a bow.

My lovely mother, my bestest friend in the whole wide world, mummy and teacher, nurse and together until the end. Now we're apart; 121 miles to be precise, I'd still come; and bugger the price, to stop you crying to stop you sighing about saying that word that feels like our love is dying. I miss you Mummy, and I don't care what people may think or feel, I don't want to say goodbye, I pretend it isn't real.

But I remember someone once saying something that seemed to stick, and even when some nosey prick, annoys me and calls me a "Mummy's boy" I just smile and think of the wondrous joy; the laughter the games and the way we used to play, the sad but enjoyable rainy days. The warmth of the fire on winters nights, and the time you beat me in a snowball fight; but now you see, we’re far apart, and I feel a gap in my heart.

Goodbye may seem permanent, and farewell seems like it’s puts out the flame. But in my heart is a memory, and there you’ll always remain.

www.ingramcontent.com/pod-product-compliance
Lightning Source LLC
Chambersburg PA
CBHW051755130826
49812CB00033B/1159
* 9 7 8 9 3 5 7 6 9 9 3 0 3 *